JEFFERSON BETHKE

NEW YORK TIMES BEST-SELLING AUTHOR OF *JESUS>RELIGION*

IT'S NOT WHAT YOU THINK

WHY CHRISTIANITY IS ABOUT SO MUCH MORE THAN GOING TO HEAVEN WHEN YOU DIE

LifeWay Press ©
Nashville, TN

Published by LifeWay Press®
© 2015 Jefferson Bethke
Reprinted Nov. 2018

No part of this work may be reproduced or transmitted in any form or by any means,
electronic or mechanical, including photocopying and recording, or by any information
storage or retrieval system, except as may be expressly permitted in writing by the publisher.
Requests for permission should be addressed in writing to
LifeWay Press, One LifeWay Plaza, Nashville, TN 37234.

ISBN: 978-1-4300-5255-5
Item number: 005782005

Dewey Decimal Classification Number: 248.83
Subject Heading: JESUS CHRIST \ CHRISTIAN LIFE \ GRACE (THEOLOGY)

Printed in the United States of America

Student Ministry Publishing
LifeWay Resources
One LifeWay Plaza
Nashville, TN 37234

We believe that the Bible has God for its author; salvation for its end;
and truth, without any mixture of error, for its matter
and that all Scripture is totally true and trustworthy.
To review LifeWay's doctrinal guideline,
please visit *www.lifeway.com/doctrinalguideline*.

CONTENTS

ABOUT JEFF

Jeff currently lives in Maui with his wife Alyssa and one-year-old daughter, Kinsley. He is the author of the books, *Jesus>Religion* and *It's Not What You Think*.

Besides writing he makes Youtube® videos, which have been seen collectively 62,000,000 times, and hosts a podcast with his wife that can be found on iTunes®.

His passion is to see people follow Jesus and come to a true life-giving understanding of the free grace of God for us all. He also has a yellow lab named Aslan and enjoys reading good books and drinking good coffee on his down time.

Jeff would love to hear about you and your story as it pertains to this Bible study. Feel free to share, critique, question, or just say hello. His contact information is below. And use #INWYTbook to share any thoughts with the world.

TWITTER	*www.twitter.com/jeffersonbethke*
INSTAGRAM	*www.instagram.com/jeffersonbethke*
PINTEREST	*www.pinterest.com/jeffersonbethke*
FACEBOOK	*www.facebook.com/jeffersonbethkepage*
YOUTUBE	*www.youtube.com/bball1989*
BLOG	*www.jeffbethke.com*

STORY

"Follow Me" is a call to be involved in a deeper, bigger story where life and joy are found.

START

What is your favorite movie?

Why is it your favorite?

Probably for most of us, our favorite movie involves a great story. There's something about a good story that draws you in and captivates you. This happens for us at all ages.

What is your favorite story from childhood?

Why is this your favorite story?

In your opinion, what makes a great story?

Have you ever thought of the Bible as a big story? Why or why not?

In this first session, we're going to focus on how we view the Bible and why that shapes our understanding of everything else in life. Keep the following question in mind as we begin this Bible study and watch the first video.

How does the way I view the Bible affect my life?

WATCH

Use the space below to take notes as you watch the video for Session 1.

CONSIDER THIS

> A lot of us come to Scripture with preconceived notions about what it is.

> How you see Scripture defines how you see God, which then defines how you see yourself.

> The best way to view Scripture is as a story.

> You matter, but you're not the center of the story.

> In Jesus' call of "Follow Me," there is a call to be involved in a deeper, bigger story where life and joy are found.

REMEMBER THIS

>

>

>

>

LOOK THIS UP

> Ephesians 6:17
> Hebrews 4:12
> Genesis 3:24; 12:1-3
> Exodus 19:6
> Isaiah 53
> Matthew 4:19

ENCOUNTER

Let's review the video by discussing the following questions:

To which of the limited views that Jeff shared about the Bible (sword, road map to life, etc.) can you best relate?

In what other ways have you had a limited view of Scripture?

How does the way you view the Bible affect the way you see God? How you see yourself?

If you see the Bible as a grand story, how does that affect the way you read Scripture? The way you see God? The way you see yourself?

Every good story has a main character. Sometimes we tend to read the Bible and make ourselves the main character. We want to make the Scripture about us, our needs, and our agenda. However, as Jeff says, you matter, but the main character in the story of Scripture is God.

What negative consequences could result from seeing ourselves at the center of Scripture's story?

How does seeing God as the center of this Scripture story help us understand His character and His purpose? And how does that ultimately help us understand our purpose?

Jeff said that "He who tells the best story wins," and that your life is a story. What is the point and interest of the story your life is telling?

Jeff mentioned the theme in Genesis of people moving east and west. Are you currently:
a) Moving east, away from God's authority.
b) Moving west, seeking God's presence.
c) Moving back and forth, wrestling with what you want.

Would you say you are running, drifting, limping, or wandering toward or away from God? Why did you describe your spiritual walk this way?

Read Matthew 4:18-20.

Jesus invited these fisherman to join Him in the bigger story. Up to that point, they were fishermen going about their jobs everyday. But Jesus pointed them to a higher purpose.

How is being a Christian not just about going to heaven when you die, but also about following Jesus into a bigger story here and now?

Jesus called men who were ordinary and even overlooked by the religious leaders of their day. How is that encouraging to you?

RESPOND

As Jesus calls you to the bigger story, how will you respond?

On the following pages are three days of personal reading and reflection. Complete these before your next group session.

PERSONAL READING AND REFLECTION

Your Starting Point

Imagine that you're looking at the still surface of glassy water.

Get a clear picture in your mind and describe it below.

Now imagine something in your hand. It could be any shape or size. Picture the scene as the object falls, drips, or is thrown into the water. As something breaks the still water and disturbs the reflections across the surface, what happens? What sound is made? How does the water move and for how long?

No matter how big or small something is, no matter how loud or quiet the splash is, when something hits the surface of water, ripples are made. These concentric circles get bigger and bigger, reaching farther and farther, going on forever until an opposing force like friction, gravity, or another object like a boundary stops them.

According to NASA, "Newton's first law states that every object will remain at rest or in uniform motion in a straight line unless compelled to change its state by the action of an external force. This is normally taken as the definition of inertia." [1]

OK. Great. So, what's the point of this little mental exercise and science lesson?

What if I told you that your view of the Bible had a ripple effect? It's the starting point from which everything else we're going to look at flows. The way you see the Bible affects the way you see God, the way you see yourself. Really, the way you respond keeps rippling into the way you see everything else in life (and beyond).

So, let's be sure to get a clear picture of what the Bible is. In the video from the group session, we looked at a simple grid that showed this ripple effect. Look at some of the examples below of how this chain reaction can play out.

Bible	God	You
Sword	Captain	Warrior
Road map	Direction-giver	Traveler
Promise book	Gift-giver	Gift-getter
Rule book	Judge	Game-player
Law	King	Citizen
Story	Author	Part of story

1 *https://www.grc.nasa.gov/www/K-12/airplane/newton.html*

In your own words, explain the way you see the Bible. Use as many words as needed in the space below.

Now let's try summarizing what you just wrote into a single word or phrase. Write it in the first space below.

_____ | _____ | _____

OK. If that is how you see the Bible, what does that make God (according to that perspective)? Write a word or phrase in the second space above.

Finally, if that is how you see the Bible and God, what does that make you (according to that perspective)? Write that word or phrase in the third space above.

What do you think of the ripple effect flowing out from your starting point? Had you ever thought through this before? Do you like what this reveals about God and your life? Write your thoughts in the space below.

Honestly, do you enjoy reading the Bible?   Yes   No   Sometimes

When and where do you most enjoy reading it?

Why is that a good time and place for reading the Bible?

Why do you read your Bible? If you don't read it often (or ever), why not?

All of the ideas in the chart have at least some truth to them. The Bible is multi-faceted, like a diamond. There are many angles from which one can see parts of it, but ultimately it's one, big, beautiful story. These other perspectives are sub-narratives, or smaller parts of the big story, the meta-narrative.

What better starting point than looking at what the Bible says about itself? Let's see how these things fit together to give us a full picture of how to read (and respond to) the Bible.

Read 2 Timothy 3:16-17.

How do these verses describe the Bible?

What does it say about the usefulness of Scripture and how we are to respond to it?

The phrase "inspired by God" or "God-breathed" describes the power and nature of Scripture as God's Word. The Bible isn't just words about God. The Bible is God's Word to us. We'll look more at the power of God's Word in the next part, but for now, let that amazing reality sink in—God is speaking to you through the Bible. He is telling you something. He is letting you know Who He is and who you are. He is telling you the great story that has been unfolding since before time began and will continue into eternity.

Take a minute to write out your thoughts or a prayer reflecting on the awesome truth that God can speak to you today and every day through His Word—the Bible.

The Power of God's Word

"In the beginning God ..." (Gen. 1:1)

These are the very first words of the first sentence on the first page of the first book of the Bible. By the way, the Bible is one big story, but it is made up of 66 books. Think of it like a series. Right away we can see that this story is (and always has been) about God.

Read Genesis 1:1–2:3.

What does this opening scene of Scripture describe?

Notice the phrase repeated at the beginning of verses 3, 6, 9, 14, 20, 24, and 26. How did God create everything?

Several repeated phrases in this scene give us incredible insight into the main character.

Write down the number of times you see the following words in Genesis 1:1–2:3 (or similar words, depending on your translation).
"God"   "said"   "it was so"   "it was good"   "blessed"

What does this reveal about God and His Word?

It's pretty amazing to think about the formless and empty darkness becoming everything we experience through our senses today. It all came into being in response to God's voice. Darkness was filled with light. Emptiness was filled with life.

DAY TWO

C. S. Lewis describes a scene like this in *The Magician's Nephew*, the first book of his classic series *The Chronicles of Narnia*. In that fictional creation account, Aslan the lion is king and creator of the world known as Narnia. He creates everything by singing over the space and the tone of his voice sends ripples of life as everything bubbles up and springs into existence in the wake of his song.

The point of Genesis is less about how exactly physical matter works and more about the good, powerful, and wise Creator—God. Everything is under His authority. His power is absolute. His Word has authority. His design is good.

Even Jesus quoted the following Scripture from the Old Testament when tempted to use His miraculous power to make food for Himself during a season of intense prayer and fasting:

> *"It is written, 'Man must not live on bread alone but on every word that comes from the mouth of God.'" (Matt. 4:4)*

To get the full power of this statement (or any verse in the Bible), it helps to consider the context. These words are profound in and of themselves, but keep in mind that Jesus was tempted to turn stones into bread after not eating anything for 40 days! When Jesus quoted Deuteronomy 8:3, He essentially said that He could give up physical needs for a long period of time, but couldn't give up trust in and obedience to God's Word for even a moment.

How would you describe the necessity of God's Word?

Jesus demonstrated that the Word of God is powerful in guarding our lives from spiritual attack and fighting temptation. The Bible describes God's Word as our sword (Eph. 6:17). Again, it's important to keep context in mind as this imagery for God's Word is in the context of spiritual warfare; it's not a weapon to be used against other people (Eph. 6:12).

One other time the Bible compares itself to a sword is in the Book of Hebrews.

Read Hebrews 4:12-13.

Here the imagery is personal accountability. The sword is like a scalpel, revealing what's inside our hearts. Again, the purpose is spiritual, but in this case, it is God wielding the sword, not us. It's a picture of God's absolute authority, power, wisdom, and justice.

How would you describe the sword imagery of God's Word?

How has reading and knowing Scripture helped you when facing temptation? How has Scripture convicted you of sin in your heart?

It's important to understand that God's Word is not just functional, but it is a source of joy. Read all of Psalm 119. There you'll see the infinite goodness of God's Word. The whole chapter is an acrostic poem (meaning each new section begins with the next letter of the Hebrew alphabet) about the value of and joy in Scripture.

For now, end your time thanking God for giving you His Word.

A Bigger And Better Story

Ever set up dominoes in a figure or pattern? If so, you know that one little bump sets the whole thing off.

In the first section, you saw the domino effect (or ripple effect) with your view of the Bible. The way you see the Bible affects the way you see God, which then affects the way you see yourself. They all flow into one another. Once one idea starts leaning in one direction, everything else follows.

The trajectory of your life will continue in its current direction unless something stops you and changes your direction. The story of the Bible shows a pattern of people falling away from God and how He interrupted our downward spiral of self-destruction.

In the second section, you saw that God created everything in heaven and on earth by the power of His Word. Then God looked at everything, blessed it, and said that it was good. Everything was in perfect balance, harmony, and rhythm. But then something happened. The order of the universe tipped and made a mess of everything.

Genesis 3 describes the familiar story of Adam and Eve's disobedience in the garden of Eden. You might think that the original sin was eating the forbidden fruit. That is partly true. That was the visible action that broke the one and only rule God provided. God had established a healthy boundary in His goodness and the man, woman, and all of creation was flourishing.

The problem began the instant they entertained the idea that God shouldn't be trusted and that He wasn't really good. They wondered if there was a bigger and better story than the one God was telling them. They gave into the temptation of seeking happiness apart from God and the way He designed life to work. Despite this epic tragedy that introduced sin into the world, we see glimmers of hope.

Read Genesis 3.

Describe Adam and Eve's immediate response to their sin (Gen. 3:7-8).

Describe God's immediate response. (See Gen. 3:9.)

What does God's presence and question reveal about Him?

From that point, we see human relationships break as Adam and Eve started passing the blame, neither one owning up to their responsibility for the defiant act. Consequences and curses shatter the entire created order. Sin has fractured everything to its core.

But in His goodness, God called out for them, and He sacrificially provided clothing to cover their shame. He mercifully guarded them from the tree of life so that they would not be separated forever from a personal relationship with Him.

Underline, circle, or highlight the direction mentioned in each verse as human history begins unraveling from this point.

He drove man out and stationed the cherubim and the flaming, whirling sword east of the garden of Eden to guard the way to the tree of life. (Gen. 3:24)

Then Cain went out from the Lord's presence and lived in the land of Nod, east of Eden. (Gen. 4:16)

After Adam and Eve's sin, they were banished to the east. After their son, Cain, sinned, he was banished east. From that point, Genesis describes the growing brokenness of humanity with the sole exception of a faithful family line from Adam, through another son, Seth, to Noah, to Abram, who would become Abraham (Gen. 3-12). Abram, in contrast to this general trend moved from Ur (near the Persian Gulf) to Canaan (near the Mediterranean Sea) and even temporarily into Egypt—a general trend of moving west.

We don't need to overspiritualize and exaggerate the action of literally moving in any direction, but it is a symbolic pattern in the story of Genesis that sets up a major theme in Scripture—running from God or following Him in faith.

Let's think again about a question from the group session. According to this pattern in Genesis, are you currently:
> **Moving east, away from God's authority.**
> **Moving west, seeking God's presence.**
> **Moving back and forth, wrestling with what you want.**

How would you describe your movement in relation to God?
running   limping   wandering   other:

Why did you describe your spiritual journey this way?

God invited Abraham to join the story He had been telling since the beginning, one of mercy and love and blessing. Unlike Adam, who hid in shame when God called, Abraham responded in faith, following God even when He didn't understand where He was going.

Read Hebrews 11:1-19.

What word was repeated over and over as the obvious theme in that summary of biblical history?

According to verses 2 and 6, how would you describe the importance of faith?

Abraham trusted what God said. He lived on earth as a citizen of a heaven. This is going to be a major theme throughout the story of Scripture and in this Bible study. Abraham's story of living by faith, even with the life of his son Isaac, ultimately pointed to Jesus. Every story in Hebrews 11 (and in the entire Bible) points to Jesus.

When Jesus called His disciples, they too were ordinary people who had to trust that He was truly inviting them into a bigger and better story than the one they were living. That's what faith is—acting on your belief in God. It's responding to his invitation to join Him in a bigger and better story.

Read Matthew 4:18-22.

How do stories of ordinary people living by faith encourage you? Are there any other stories of people in history or in your life that inspire you to trust God's Word and to live by faith? If so, whom?

Imagine if someone were writing your biography or making a documentary film, what would your life story be about?

If your story is about anything other than following God's call, if anything else is at the center of your life, what needs to change so that you point to Jesus?

There's a tension in a life of faith. You matter, but you're not the center of the story. Your life is not about you. This is actually an incredibly freeing reality. Unlike Adam and Eve, who fell for the lie that there was a better story than the one God had given them, everyone who lives by faith and follows Jesus enters the story God has been telling since day one. In His own words, Jesus told those He had called to follow Him exactly why He came.

"I have come so that they may have life and have it in abundance." (John 10:10)

TEMPLE

God wants to dwell in us and He pursues us with His mercy and love.

START

Session 1 focused on the domino effect of how our view of Scripture impacts our view of God and of ourselves.

What was most helpful, encouraging, or challenging from your personal reading and reflection in Session 1?

Today we'll focus more on how the big story of Scripture is about pursuit and relationship.

Have you ever gone to great lengths to get something or to be with someone? Explain.

Why would someone be willing to pursue something or someone, even at great personal cost?

Keep the following question in mind as we watch the next video.

If the story of the Bible is true, how will you respond?

WATCH

Use the space below to take notes as you watch the video for Session 2.

CONSIDER THIS

⟩ From the first page, we see that the dwelling place of God is the entire earth.

⟩ God doesn't want to be confined to a building or a space. He wants to flood the earth with His presence.

⟩ In Jesus, God "pitched His tent" with His people (John 1:14).

⟩ God in the temple, God in Jesus, now through the Spirit, God in us.

⟩ You don't have an option to be stagnant. God is descending in the narrative of Scripture. Will you receive that or turn around and say no?

REMEMBER THIS

⟩

⟩

⟩

⟩

LOOK THIS UP

⟩ Genesis 1:27
⟩ Exodus 29:45-46; 32:8-9
⟩ John 1:1; 1:14
⟩ Acts 2:1-4
⟩ 1 Corinthians 3:16
⟩ Revelation 21:22
⟩ Habakkuk 2:14
⟩ Psalm 47:8
⟩ Hebrews 12:2

ENCOUNTER

How does the reality of the whole earth being filled with God's presence affect the way you see your daily life?

Read Genesis 1:27.

How does being created in the image of God affect your view of God? Of yourself? The way you interact with others?

How did God continue to descend in pursuit of a relationship with us?

Read 1 Corinthians 3:16.

If you are a Christian, how does having the Spirit inside of you change the way you live?

How does seeing Him as pursuing you change your view of God? How does it require a response from you?

RESPOND

Jeff asked how you would respond to God's pursuit of a relationship with you through Jesus. How have you responded to His call?

On the following pages are three days of personal reading and reflection. Complete these before your next group session.

PERSONAL READING AND REFLECTION

DAY ONE

Made in His Image

Let's do a quick review. In the previous session you saw these three major points:

> Your starting point is going to have a ripple effect, influencing the overall direction of your life. The way you approach the Bible will shape your view of God and of yourself.

> The Bible is God's Word. God created everything by the power of His command. As Creator, He has absolute authority and knows what is best for our happiness.

> Humans have consistently turned from God's loving authority and sought happiness apart from Him. But the Bible tells a story of how God calls broken people back to abundant life through faith in Jesus.

This week we'll look at these major points:

> People are unique among all of God's creation.

> God didn't take any shortcuts in making Himself known and in making a relationship with Him possible.

> Life changes radically when you understand that God doesn't live off in some distant corner of outer space called heaven. He isn't limited to sacred buildings or places either.

When you read the creation story in the previous session you may have noticed another pattern that we didn't mention.

What do the following verses say were created "according to their kinds" or "according to its kind" in Genesis 1?
> **Verse 11**
> **Verse 12**
> **Verse 21**
> **Verse 24**
> **Verse 25**

But the pattern breaks in the story, drawing added emphasis to the unique nature of this particular part of God's good creation.

> *Then God said, "Let Us make man in Our image, according to Our likeness. They will rule the fish of the sea, the birds of the sky, the livestock, all the earth, and the creatures that crawl on the earth." So God created man in His own image;*
> *He created him in the image of God; He created them male and female. (Gen. 1:26-27)*

Underline the words *image* and *likeness* in Genesis 1:26-27.

Circle every reference to God (including: God, Us, Our, His, He, and own) in Genesis 1:26-27.

Draw a box around every reference to humans (including: man, him, them, male, and female) in Genesis 1:26-27.

What does this say about the unique nature of human beings?

How is it encouraging to you personally? How is it convicting?

In what ways do you see people turning away from what God's Word says about human beings, both male and female, being created uniquely in the image and likeness of God?

If you trust God's Word, believing that people are created in His image, how does it change the way you see and relate to God?

Sin distorts the likeness of God in us, like a mirror from a clown house at a carnival. We haven't lost the image of God, but it is broken. As a result, we can never relate properly to God or to anyone or anything else He created, no matter how hard we try.

Read Romans 12:22-23.

What things have you turned to for happiness instead of God?

Anything you turn to instead of God is an idol. It's easy to dismiss verses that mention idols since you probably don't pray to physical images of a deity, but putting yourself or anything else God created as the focal point of your life is sin—it's idolatry.

You were made in the image of God. He designed you to reflect His goodness, His righteousness, and His glorious likeness to the world around you.

Ask God to help you turn your focus to Him in faith. Ask for His forgiveness for any idolatry in your heart and thank Him for the goodness He's revealed to you through His Word.

God With Us

On December 25, we celebrate one of the most unexpected and pivotal moments in all of history. An unwed, teenage virgin gave birth to God in the flesh. It is a key part of the story God has been telling since the beginning of time.

It was and still is unusual, to say the least, to believe in a deity who is all-powerful, all-knowing, ever-present, yet also vulnerable, pursuing us, serving us, and even dying for us.

It's easy to take for granted the extraordinary nature of the story of God as revealed in Scripture. Let's trace the steps of God as He continually humbled Himself, coming down to be among His people.

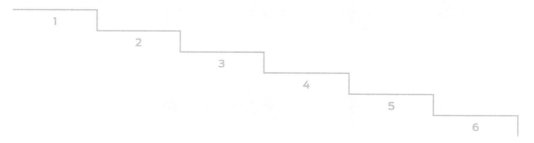

In the session 2 video teaching, Genesis was described as beginning with a "temple building text." In the story of creation you see God creating three environments on days 1-3, filling those environments on days 4-6, placing God's image within His creation, and then declaring a holy time of rest and celebration on the seventh day.

DAY 1	DAY 2	DAY 3
Light & Dark	*Sea & Sky*	*Land & Vegetation*
DAY 4	**DAY 5**	**DAY 6**
Sun, Moon & Stars	*Fish, Sea Creatures & Birds*	*Land Creatures & Human Beings*

DAY 7
Holy day of rest and blessing

From the very beginning, God has intended to dwell among His people.

On the top step write "Heaven and Earth."

How does it shape the way you see life to think that God created the world—both time and space—as a holy place to be with us?

God is not a distant creator. He wants to be with us and has never stopped pursuing us. Even after mankind rebelled, He continually called people into relationship with Him.

Read Exodus 29:45-46 and 40:34-38.

On the second step (p. 24) write "The Tabernacle."

Why is it significant that God had a visible presence among an entire community of people as they followed Him? What does that reveal about God? How would it benefit people?

Read 1 Kings 8:14-20 and 9:1-9

On the third step (p. 24) write "The Temple."

Why was it significant for God to have a consistent presence among His people? What does that reveal about God? How would it benefit people?

Read John 1:1-5 and 14.

On the fourth step (p. 24) write "Jesus."

Why is it significant that God became a man—that the Creator was not only in His creation, but also part of it? What does that reveal about God? How would it benefit people?

Read Acts 2:1-4, 17-23, and 37-40.

On the fifth step (p. 24) write "The Holy Spirit."

Why is it significant that God gives His Spirit to those who believe in Him? What does that reveal about God? How would it benefit people?

Read Revelation 21:1-5 and 22-27.

On the sixth and final step (p. 24) write "New Heaven and Earth."

Why is it significant that God have a visible presence among His people, as they followed Him? What does this reveal about God? How does it excite you and give you hope?

If you really want to be blown away, read the following chapters to see how God cares about every little detail when it comes to our relationship with Him. (Creation: Genesis 1-2; Tabernacle: Exodus 25-31 and 35-40; Temple: 1 Kings 5-9; Our Future: Revelation 21-22.)

It's overwhelming to consider the attention God gives to each detail. In the last passage you read describing our future, you see a bride being presented to a groom. God's care for the details is like a loving Father, providing for His family and wanting everything to be perfect in celebration of the joy and love between Christ and His people—the Church.

In Acts 37-40, Peter said that everyone has to decide whether or not they will put their faith in Jesus. By faith God then gives His Spirit. Everyone who has the Spirit will live forever in the joyful presence of God the Father, Jesus the Son, and all of His people.

Reflect on the amazing reality that over the course of human history God has been pursuing a relationship with His people. Realize that He has specifically pursued a personal relationship with you. Express your response below.

Describe the moment you realized God was pursuing you and how you responded to Him through faith in Jesus.

A Living Temple

The tabernacle and the temple were visible, tangible places of worship and evidence of God's presence among His people. Extreme attention to detail was given for who could interact with the sacred spaces and how it was to be done. These beautifully ornate places were a source of great joy and hope for God's people. It was something that the whole world could see, recognizing them as a community of individuals identified by faith in God.

But when Jesus entered the story as God in the flesh, everything was changing. The temple and the religious practices surrounding it had become a source of arrogant pride and division. Jesus took everyone's understanding of the temple and turned it upside down when He declared:

> *"Destroy this sanctuary, and I will raise it up in three days." (John 2:19)*

Read John 2:13-22.

What new meaning to sanctuary or temple did Jesus introduce?

What evidence did Jesus give for His passion against man-centered religion and for a God-centered life?

How are you sometimes distracted by meaningless (and possibly even divisive) self-centered religion?

What would it look like for Jesus to chase out selfish religion in your own heart? What would He get rid of and overturn?

While Jesus was physically walking the earth, He was the sacred place where heaven and earth met. He was the intersection of the holy and human. He was 100 percent God and 100 percent man. He was the true temple. As revolutionary as this was, He made an even more radical (and at the time, even more confusing) promise.

Read John 14:1-12.

Just like God had a very specific way to approach Him in the tabernacle and the temple, what did Jesus say was the only way to enter into a personal and eternal relationship with God?

Read John 16:5-13.

What did Jesus promise His followers?

Have you ever felt that believing in and following God would be easier if you could see and hear Him? Why would that be better?

Why did Jesus say it is actually for our benefit that He is not with us in a physical body any more?

Jesus told His followers that they would be able to do even more than He did while He was with them because they would be empowered by the same Spirit. Even basic math tells us that millions of Christians can accomplish more than one Jesus in human form. Now you may be thinking, "But I'm not Jesus!" True. But Jesus says we all have the same Spirit. That's pretty amazing. Let this truth sink in. Jesus said it is for your good and for His glory that He gives you the Spirit instead of His physical presence on earth.

Don't you yourselves know that you are God's sanctuary and that the Spirit of God lives in you? (1 Cor. 3:16)

Have you ever thought of yourself as a temple?   Yes   No

How does it change the way you view your life to know that the Spirit of God—the same Spirit Jesus had—lives in you?

How does it change the way you view other believers as temples of God's Spirit dwelling within them?

How does it change what you desire for nonbelievers to realize that though they have a broken image of God in them, they do not have His Spirit?

This isn't just symbolic language about Jesus being in your heart. The Bible says several times that the Spirit of God is literally within the people who put their faith in Jesus. When God first sent the Spirit there was clear evidence of this fact. Throughout the Book of Acts the constant theme is the evidence and power of the Holy Spirit in the lives of Christians.

It's easy to think of the Spirit in abstract or symbolic terms, if we think about Him at all. So let's look at some very practical realities about the Holy Spirit.

Read 1 Corinthians 6:12-20.

What does this passage say about the spiritual nature of physical activities like eating, drinking, and sexual behavior?

Draw a line to match each phrase with the Scripture describing the Spirit's work. (These are just a few—there's so many more!)

1. John 16:8	a. testify that you are God's child
2. John 16:13-14	b. seal us in salvation
3. Acts 1:8 and 4:31	c. give life
4. Romans 8:2	d. empower to share the gospel
5. Romans 8:16	e. convict of sin & righteousness
6. Romans 8:26	f. guide into all truth
7. 1 Corinthians 2:13	g. free you from sin & death
8. 2 Corinthians 1:22	h. understand spiritual truth
9. 2 Corinthians 3:6	i. help you pray for what you need

(Answers below.)

Finally let's look at the personal character of a person filled with the Spirit. In the space below write each trait mentioned in Galatians 5:22-23 described as fruit of the Spirit.

Close by praying that God would grow the fruit of the Spirit in your life, making you more like Jesus. Thank Him for the many ways the Spirit is at work in and through you.

(1-e, 2-f, 3-d, 4-g, 5-a, 6-i, 7-h, 8-b, 9-c)

SESSION THREE

KINGDOM

Rather than fleeing the world, Jesus calls us to be the light in the world spreading His love on earth.

START

Session 2 focused on how God has continuously pursued a personal relationship with His people.

What was most helpful, encouraging, or challenging from your personal reading and reflection in Session 2?

Now we'll shift our attention to the disruptive nature of the gospel.

When have you caused a disturbance—intentionally or accidentally? Briefly share stories.

Nobody expected God to enter history in the person of Jesus. Today we'll see how disruptive it was for the King of the universe to enter the world He created. Keep the following question in mind as you watch the next video.

Who or what is in the place of authority over your life?

WATCH

Use the space below to take notes as you watch the video for Session 3.

CONSIDER THIS

⟩ When Jesus claimed the titles, "King of Kings," "Lord of Lords," and "Son of God," for Himself, He was making a major statement about who He was and who Caesar was not.

⟩ More than just talking about a kingdom to come, Jesus was saying that He was Lord now. This was a major shift in the first century culture.

⟩ The temple represents that middle place where heaven and earth collide.

⟩ Jesus is the tabernacle or temple for believers (John 1:14; 2:19).

⟩ Rather than fleeing the world, Jesus calls us to be the light in the world spreading His love on earth.

REMEMBER THIS

⟩

⟩

⟩

⟩

⟩

LOOK THIS UP

⟩ Luke 22:70
⟩ John 1:14; 2:19; 13:3-17; 13:35; 18:37
⟩ Matthew 4:17; 5:39-45; 6:10; 20:28
⟩ 1 Thessalonians 5:18

ENCOUNTER

How are Christians known—what is their reputation?

Read John 13:34-35.

How would you describe the love of Christ?

How would the perception of Christians change if we were known for Christlike love—even for enemies? What, specifically, would change in your life?

Read Matthew 5:38-47.

How does it reveal our identities as citizens of a different kingdom and as children of a Heavenly Father to live with such radical love?

How is the love of Christ unlike the so-called love and good deeds of the world?

When have you had to love someone who was difficult to love? When has someone shown you unnatural kindness that you didn't deserve?

RESPOND

Jeff concluded by asking two takeaway questions:
   a) Are you letting the rule of Jesus order your priorities?
   b) Are you going out as a kingdom citizen to show people the greatness of our King?

What specific and practical examples can you share for the two questions above?

On the following pages are three days of personal reading and reflection. Complete these before your next group session.

PERSONAL READING AND REFLECTION

The King's Good News

Let's start again with a quick review of what we covered last time:

- People, both male and female, are unique among God's creation. We are made in His image. Sin distorted the image of God and all of creation was broken as a result of sin.
- God didn't abandon us in our sinful condition to live and die apart from Him forever. He has constantly pursued a relationship with people called out to live by faith. The way He related to His people became increasingly more vulnerable and personal in nature. Eventually we'll live in a perfectly restored heaven and earth with God.
- Life changes radically when you understand that God is not a distant God. He isn't limited to sacred buildings or places. You are the temple of His Spirit—the same Spirit that raised Jesus from the dead lives inside of you and every Christian.

When you grasp God's story, you start to understand what it really means to live as part of His kingdom, not just in heaven when you die, but right here and now on earth.

You also begin to see that as one created in the image of God and filled with His Spirit, the greatest need of everyone around you is to join this epic drama and life-giving reality. The Spirit conforms you more and more into the likeness of Jesus as you continue His mission of inviting other people into a right relationship with God.

Let's start unpacking this idea of the kingdom by looking first at the word *gospel*.

What do you think of when you hear the word *gospel*?

Who first explained the gospel to you? How did they explain it?

Gospel, to most of us, means a religious message about Jesus or the books of the Bible specifically about Jesus (Matthew, Mark, Luke, and John). According to Merriam-Webster®, another contemporary meaning is that gospel is synonymous with absolute truth. In other words, somebody might say "Football is gospel" meaning that particular item, experience, or event is most important, or "the gospel according to my coach," giving primary importance to the coach's words. Ironically, even that cultural usage is based on the life story of Jesus being absolutely true.

What was the meaning of "gospel" in Jesus' day? Look at the opening lines to the Gospel of Mark, which is agreed by most scholars to be the first Gospel written (65-70 A.D.).

The beginning of the gospel of Jesus Christ, the Son of God. As it is
written in Isaiah the prophet: Look, I am sending My messenger ahead
of You, who will prepare Your way. A voice of one crying out in the wilderness:
Prepare the way for the Lord; make His paths straight! (Mark 1:1-3)

The word gospel is from *euangelion* in Greek or *evangelion* in Latin, meaning "good news." The word wasn't unique to Christians. It wasn't even originally a religious word. It first was used by rulers, in particular Caesar and the Roman empire. When good news was spread throughout the empire of a great victory or of a new Caesar, it would be proclaimed (*evangelizo*) by messengers (where we get our word, evangelists).

This was the culture and context into which Jesus entered and in which the message of His life, victory over death, salvation and kingdom were first preached, written down, and spread throughout the land.

How does the word *evangelize* now relate to Jesus?

Caesar Augustus founded the Roman Empire shortly before the birth of Jesus (Luke 2:1). His stepson, Tiberius Caesar was emperor during the ministry, crucifixion, and resurrection of Jesus and during the earliest days of the Christian church (See Luke 3:1.). Specifically regarding the time the Gospel of Mark was written, Nero, the great-great-grandnephew of Augustus was emperor and began officially and infamously persecuting Christians.

The Caesars in power as the story of Jesus unfolded claimed the titles "Son of the Divine" "King of kings" and "Lord of lords." Evangelists spread "good news" throughout the empire about Caesar to maintain order, establish peace, and celebrate mighty victories.

Do you see how dangerously subversive the language of the gospel story of Jesus was at the time? What has become religious jargon was loaded with revolutionary language. Do you remember what Jesus was asked by the Roman leader, how He was mocked, what was written on His cross, and then what the Roman soldier said after His death?

Read Mark 15:2,17-18,26,39.

To follow Jesus meant declaring your allegiance to a king other than Caesar and a kingdom that was not Rome. It was to declare that Jesus was the truly Divine Son, King of kings, and Lord of lords. To evangelize others, spreading the good news of His victory over death from sin and the coming of His heavenly kingdom to earth was radical to say the least.

But the gospel of Jesus is so much bigger than any earthly political empire or military victory. Bigger than the legalistic box in which religion had tried to keep God. Jesus was setting people free from sin and death. Look at Jesus' first words in the Gospel of Mark.

"The time is fulfilled, and the kingdom of God has come near. Repent and believe in the good news!" (Mark 1:15)

From what do you need to repent?

Practically, what does it look like for you in the 21st century to believe in the good news that Jesus is your King?

If the gospel was as radical in our culture today as it was 2,000 years ago (and still is in some parts of the world), would you still follow Jesus?

Ambassadors of the King

If you've ever wondered what your purpose is in life or what you're supposed to "do" as a Christian, here's some great news. You've been given a mission.

Read Matthew 28:18-20.

Read the first and last sentences again. How are those words encouraging?

This passage is often referred to as The Great Commission. It wasn't just Jesus' final words for His disciples in that moment. It also applies to every believer. Your job, as part of the kingdom, is to go make other disciples.

But Jesus' disciples didn't get it. These guys had been with Jesus for three years of teaching and miracles, seen Him killed, buried, and resurrected for 40 days, and the very last thing they ask Him misses the point.

Read Acts 1:6-8. What was their question?

How did they miss the point?

When you begin to understand how subversive and threatening to the status quo the gospel of Jesus and the kingdom of God originally was, hopefully an excited (and maybe a good kind of nervous) passion starts burning in you like a fire.

The gospel is still that radical, changing everything. However, our familiarity with it causes us to lose sight of it's power. People still need to hear it. You needed it, right?

Read Jeremiah 20:9. How did Jeremiah describe knowing the truth?

Read Acts 4:20. How did two of Jesus' followers describe it?

How would you describe your passion and enthusiasm to share the gospel of God's kingdom?

On a scale of 1-10, 1 being never and 10 being constantly, how often do you talk about Jesus?

| 1 | 2 | 3 | 4 | 5 | 6 | 7 | 8 | 9 | 10 |

If you don't talk about Jesus often, why not?

If you do, what do you most enjoy talking about?

Read 2 Corinthians 5:17-21.

As part of God's kingdom you have been given a new identity; what is it according to this Scripture?

To reconcile means to make things right. We've been reconciled to God through Jesus. Now we join the work in bringing everything and everyone back under the rule of our King. Not by force or manipulation (that's the way of the world), but by the power of the gospel and our witness in word and deed. We are ambassadors, continuing the work Jesus began. This means that when He says He has all authority and then sends us out, promising to always be with us by His Spirit, then we now have His power and authority to act on behalf of the kingdom.

Remember, in the beginning God created heaven and earth in perfect harmony. There was *shalom* (the Hebrew word meaning peace). We could think of it like this:

HEAVEN
EARTH

Sin broke everything (Gen. 3). *Shalom* was shattered. It's common, but wrong, to think of earth and physical things as bad and heaven and spiritual things as good but completely separate. Christians often mistakenly think that our job as Christians is to escape earth and get into heaven when we die.

EARTH   HEAVEN

But Christianity and the gospel is so much better than that. The Bible shows that God has constantly maintained a connection with us. There has always been a point of overlap, from the garden, to the tabernacle, to the temple, to Jesus, and now it's us. It's you. As a living temple of the Holy Spirit, you are now the point of overlap between heaven and earth, physical and spiritual.

And as an ambassador of reconciliation, your job is to bring little pockets of heaven with you, wherever you go—home, work, school, church, the street, the beach, everywhere.

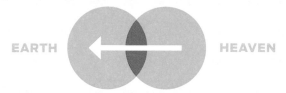

EARTH   HEAVEN

List as many places as you can think of in and around the circles above to represent where you can bring reconciliation.

In the end, God will fully restore everything and heaven and earth will be one again. But until that time, you have a mission. Jesus called people to repent, believe in the gospel, for the kingdom of heaven is near. It's nearer than you thought. It's not some detached spiritual realm we float into after we die. It's living under His authority as King right now. With His Spirit, you don't have to go across the world to be a missionary (though He might call you to do that). You can begin the Great Commission right where you are. You're an ambassador of the kingdom of heaven here on earth. Today.

How would you explain the gospel? Write a short summary of the story, including how it changed your life.

Kingdom Life

Did you notice that the mission Jesus gave His followers sounded a lot like something we saw back in Genesis? Jesus told the disciples to go make more disciples in all nations as His witnesses in Jerusalem, Judea and Samaria, and to the ends of the earth. (See Matt. 28:19 and Acts 1:8.) In the beginning God told Adam and Eve to be fruitful and multiply, filling the earth with His image and likeness (Gen. 1:28).

Making disciples is the ministry of reconciliation. Making disciples is being fruitful and multiplying.

The whole earth is to be filled with the image and likeness of God. When a king rules over a kingdom His image is spread throughout the land to represent his authority. This still happens today. In the United States, for example, you see flags, seals, symbols like the eagle, and even pictures of presidents on our money.

During the time of Jesus there was a tension among the cultures of religious Jews and the Roman Empire. Some leaders tried to force Jesus into saying something controversial. Look at His response.

Read Mark 12:13-17.

What did Jesus say belonged to the earthly government?

What did He imply belongs to the kingdom of God?

What does that look like practically? How can you give God your life today?

The *denarius* with Caesar's image on it also had a title inscribed on it declaring his authority and divinity. Jesus, the true Son of God, reminded everyone that we should give ourselves to God because we are created in His image. We represent His kingdom.

The Spirit conforms you more and more into the likeness of Jesus as you continue His mission of inviting other people into a right relationship with God. So, what does a spiritually fruitful life look like? What should be growing in you and being reproduced in others?

Read Galatians 5:22-23.

Write each fruit of the Spirit in the pieces below and answer the personal questions.

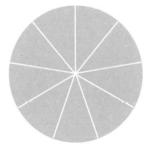

The characteristic that is hardest for me is:

I see God growing me in this area right now:

Notice that these are described as "fruit of the Spirit," not fruits. They are all pieces of the whole. When the Spirit is at work within you, you'll be conformed to the likeness of Christ in all of these characteristics. Don't get discouraged if it doesn't happen immediately. Fruit takes time to grow and there are seasons. But this is what a healthy life looks like.

Let's drill down into one of those areas right now. Though all of those characteristics are part of the same fruit, there's one that Jesus really focused on that you might think of as being the root that gives life to the rest of the fruit, or maybe the part that surrounds it all.

Read John 13:34-35.

The context of this command is important. The previous verses contain the story of Jesus washing His disciples feet, even the feet of Judas, who would betray Him, and Peter, who would deny Him. Jesus, once again, modeled God's humble love for us by literally getting down on His hands and knees to wash their feet. This was the lowest form of service in that culture. Imagine how filthy feet were in a time when most roads were dirt, most shoes were sandals, and any transportation involved animals. Jesus then willingly surrenders to those who hated Him and died sacrificially on the cross so that anyone who believes in Him can be reconciled to God and given a new life (See John 3:16).

Read the following passages and then, next to each Scripture, write words or phrases to summarize Christian love.
   > **Matthew 5:43-48**
   > **Matthew 22:34-40**
   > **1 Corinthians 13:4-7**
   > **1 John 3:16-18**
   > **1 John 5:3**

Whom do you know that is a picture of Jesus' love and can help you grow spiritually? (Write as many names as possible.)

Don't be afraid to ask that person (or people) questions or advice for how to understand and live out the truth in God's Word. Talk to them soon, maybe even right after you finish this devotion.

Who is the hardest person (or people) in your life to love?

How can you show love and forgiveness to him/her/them?

Jesus said that this countercultural love is the way the world will recognize Christians. If we're known for anything else, and honestly we have earned a pretty bad reputation as being unloving in many ways, we need to repent, ask His forgiveness, and allow the Spirit to grow healthy fruit in our lives. Remember, He desires to give us abundant life.

When you understand that you're created in the image of God and filled with His Spirit, you know that the greatest need of everyone around you is to join this life-giving reality.

With whom will you share the gospel message of love and forgiveness, helping them to be reconciled with God?

Take a moment to thank God for His amazing (and undeserved) love.

SESSION FOUR

SCARS

Jesus heals our wounds, turning them into scars that tell His story.

START

What was most helpful, encouraging, or challenging from your personal reading and reflection in Session 3?

Today we'll shift our focus to how Jesus uses our scars to tell His story.

What physical scars do you have and how did you get them? Briefly share stories.

What, if anything, did you learn from the experience when you were wounded?

Everyone gets hurt but Jesus can turn our wounds into scars. Keep the following question in mind as we watch the next video.

What wounds need healing or have been healed in your life?

WATCH

Use the space below to take notes as you watch the video for Session 4.

CONSIDER THIS

) Just like physical wounds need a doctor to tend to them, our spiritual brokenness requires Jesus—the Great Physician—to heal them (Ps. 103:3; Matt. 9:12-13).

) Once healed, our wounds become scars.

) The spiritual scars we have allow us to tell people about Jesus who heals our spiritual brokenness (2 Cor. 1:3-5).

) Jesus meets us in our pain, struggle, and doubt to assure us that He is with us in our difficulties.

REMEMBER THIS

)

)

)

)

LOOK THIS UP

) Psalm 103:3
) Matthew 9:12-13
) 2 Corinthians 1:3-5
) Leviticus 16:1-22
) Matthew 3:17
) John 20:24-29

ENCOUNTER

Jeff shared a time in his life where he was struggling and the grace he was shown was a turning point in his relationship with God. Whom has God used to show you grace and unconditional love? How did it encourage you? How did their example help you better understand a relationship with God?

What turning points have you experienced in your relationship with God?

Read John 20:24-29.

What is most encouraging to you about the way Jesus responded to Thomas? Why is that encouraging?

When have you struggled to believe something about Jesus? How did you overcome your doubt and start believing?

What questions do you still wrestle with regarding Jesus? How can you give those questions to God, trusting Him even when you can't see the answer?

What else was most helpful, encouraging, or challenging for you in the video? Why?

RESPOND

Jeff talked about how we can meet Jesus in the midst of our greatest doubt, pain, and struggle. What can you do to ensure you are trusting Jesus with the difficulties in your life?

What specific and practical ways can you begin trusting God with all of your wounds? How will you leverage the scars from your life to speak Jesus into the lives of others?

On the following pages are three days of personal reading and reflection. Complete these before your next group session.

PERSONAL READING AND REFLECTION

DAY ONE

Our Many Wounds

Review three major points from last session:

) The gospel message is radically countercultural. You are called to live as part of God's kingdom now, not just in heaven when you die.

) As King with all authority, Jesus gave you a mission. You are an ambassador of His kingdom, bringing pockets of heaven on earth wherever you go.

) The Spirit conforms you more and more into the likeness of Jesus as you continue His mission of inviting other people to be reconciled to God through His love.

By now you may be thinking that this can't apply to you. You may think you're too messed up or done too many bad things to be a Christian. Or if you're already a Christian, you may think you have to settle for being on the JV squad, riding the bench as you sit on the sidelines and let the professionals share the gospel and do real ministry. But that's not an option. At least not according to Jesus and the Great Commission. You already saw that even His own disciples didn't get it right all the time and bumbled along in their journey. So you can find comfort in that fact and in these three things this week:

) We all have wounds. Some of these are self-inflicted by our own sin, other time we are injured by others' sin, and we all experience pain and suffering in broken world.

) Our God doesn't just know about our suffering; He knows what it feels like to suffer. Jesus was tempted and hurt, getting the full human experience yet never sinned.

) Because Jesus was perfect, His sacrifice was the only one that could reconcile us to God and bring true healing. In His healing God reveals a new purpose in our pain.

> *For all have sinned and fall short of the glory of God. (Rom. 3:23)*

In other words, we're all messed up. All of us are rebellious, sinful, and selfish. And falling hurts.

So understand that this week, and especially this section today may be tough. You're going to be asked to identify your hurt. Your wounds. But also know that the point of acknowledging your wounds is so that you can experience healing. Hiding or ignoring a wound only makes things worse. It's like an untreated cut on your body that begins to fester, growing more painful the longer we ignore it. Don't hide behind some religious or moral mask pretending like everything's fine. Life isn't all sunshine and Skittles, rainbows and unicorns. That's a fantasy. You need to deal with real life. Christianity is not a game of make believe and the church isn't full of perfect people. Look at Jesus' own words:

> *"The healthy don't need a doctor, but the sick do. I have not come to call the righteous, but sinners to repentance." (Luke 5:31-32)*

The first thing you have to do is admit that you have a sin problem. Identify specific sins in your life, even from today. (For example: attitudes, actions, desires, addictions, words)

What wounds have your sins caused in your own life? Be specific.

What wounds have your sins caused in other people's lives? Be specific.

So that first type of wound is self-inflicted. Your sin has consequences. It's yet another ripple effect. You experience the painful consequences of your own sin. Not only did sin break your relationship with God, it continues to hurt your day-to-day life too.

You also saw that your sin can hurt others. This leads into the second type of wound you experience—wounds inflicted on you by other people.

How have you been hurt by other people?

Read Romans 8:18-23.

Describe natural disasters or other ways the world is broken.

How have you been hurt by the brokenness of the world?

We've already seen that God created the world in perfect harmony and said that it was all good. But even the natural world suffers now from our sin. There's sickness and death, people have emotional and mental disorders, there are natural disasters and freak accidents. Everything from the core of the earth to the DNA in our bodies has been wrecked by sin.

Think of it like this. Roads are intended to work a certain way. It's not unloving to tell people to do certain things not to go a certain way. That's how things work best for the sake of everyone's good. It's loving to teach people the right way to do things and to warn them of any danger.

Imagine you're driving down the interstate and you decide you want to turn across the lanes or drive in the opposite direction. Not only do you put yourself in danger, everyone around you is at risk of being hurt also. You may seem to get away with it for a while but you're going to get hurt or even die.

Now imagine that you cause a wreck, either colliding into another person or hitting a physical structure like a bridge. Either way, there is shrapnel ripped off your vehicle or from the structure and scattered across the roadway. Other cars who come later are now in danger of running into your wreck or the damaged roadway, causing them to wreck.

Of course, you could just as easily be driving along innocently when you hit a massive crack, blowing out your tire, or being smacked by a reckless driver from any direction imaginable, or simply not being able to stop in time because you never could have imagined that you were about to run into someone else's collision that happened long before you ever got there.

Sin is like the chain reaction a multi-car pile up on the highway. It affects you, others, and even the way things are supposed to work. Everything starts breaking down. Sometimes you make bad choices. Sometimes other people make bad choices. Other times it wasn't directly related to anyone's fault; bad things just happened.

What wounds do you still have—sensitive or painful areas that you're afraid to let anyone, maybe even Jesus, get near?

What's keeping you from trusting Jesus to heal those wounds?

We all have wounds. Some self-inflicted, others inflicted by others. And we all experience pain and suffering in this broken world. But we have hope through God's healing.

Close by taking a moment to let the reality of sin, brokenness, and your wounds sink in. Then fully appreciate the good news of healing and life offered by Jesus,

---

When God was a Man

DAY TWO

Read John 3:16.

We're broken. The world is broken. But we don't have to perish, meaning our story doesn't have to end in disaster. All hope is not lost because 2,000 years ago, God provided the remedy to our sin.

Our God doesn't just know about our suffering; He knows what it feels like to suffer. Jesus was tempted and taunted, beaten and betrayed, hungry and humiliated. He lived and he died. Jesus had the full human experience, yet He never sinned.

We can't dismiss this too quickly, saying that of course He didn't sin, He was God. But He was also human, remember? Completely. 100 percent human. Flesh and bone.

The fact that God became a man and walked the same earth that you're sitting on right now is pretty incredible. He slept. He wept. He got tired. He got hurt. Just like you.

But we saw before that when Jesus was tempted to give in to do things His own way instead of trusting God's good will for His life, He resisted that human urge. He quoted the Word of God. He didn't give up when life was hard (Matt. 4:1-11). Jesus. Never. Sinned.

This is vitally important for three reasons that completely reorient the way we relate to God.

First, Jesus was the perfect man.

Read Romans 5:19.

Sin entered the world through the first man, Adam, and righteousness and reconciliation to God is made possible through the perfect man, Jesus. (See Romans 5:12-21.) Once Adam and Eve sinned every person born after that inherited a broken sinful nature.

What patterns of sin do you see in your own family? (For example: temper, addiction, bad relationships, etc.)

How have you seen a sinful inheritance in your own life? (In other words, what are your sin tendencies that you see in other family members?)

What wounds have been caused by sin in your family?

What tendencies are you hoping not to pass on to possible future children?

How can Jesus break that cycle of sin in your life?

We've all inherited a mess. But we can't blame the generations ahead of us. We've all made our own messes too.

Jesus knows this. Though He never sinned, He knows from experience what it's like to grow up in a family. Before He was born His earthly father considered divorcing His mother. Jesus was the oldest child of a teenage girl who got pregnant before she was married. Though this was miraculous in nature, it's not hard to imagine the gossipy whispers and judgmental looks about "that girl." He grew up in a poor family. We know this because besides being born in a barn and laid in a feeding trough, Mary's offering at the temple was two pigeons, the offering for someone who couldn't afford a lamb. His parents weren't perfect either. The only thing we know about Jesus' childhood is that Mary and Joseph left Him behind during their family trip and lost Him for three days when as a little kid. Even His own siblings thought He had gone crazy and was taking this whole spirituality thing too far. (See Matt. 1:18-25; Luke 1:26-38,2:21-24,2:41-50; Mark 3:20-35) This isn't to say those things are sinful, but simply to emphasize that Jesus understands tough family dynamics.

How does knowing that Jesus experienced family life and had to grow up just like anybody else make you feel?

Second, Jesus was the perfect priest.

We've seen that after sin entered the world, breaking man's relationship with God, the way God "came down" to relate to His people was in the tabernacle and temple. This holy space was where heaven and earth overlapped, so to speak. And the whole thing revolved around an incredibly detailed sacrificial system carried out by priests.

But if Jesus was already the perfect man, wasn't that enough to hit the reset button on everything? As always, God doesn't take any shortcuts. He was completely satisfying every detail. The whole story had been pointing to Him all along.

Read Hebrews 4:14-16.

While these verses may sound abstract, note the very practical conclusions presented in the first and last sentences.

How is this encouraging, especially in the midst of suffering?

What does the fact that Jesus endured faithfully and never gave in to sin tell you about temptation, trials, and suffering?

Third and finally, Jesus was the perfect sacrifice.

From the beginning of His earthly ministry to the prophetic vision of spiritual realities, the same imagery is used for Jesus as the ultimate sacrifice.

Read John 1:29.

Over and over in Revelation, a book full of prophetic imagery, Jesus is pictured as a lamb, and even as a slaughtered, sacrificial lamb. (See Rev. 5:6; 7:17; 14:10; 15:3; 19:6-9; 22:1-3.)

When Jesus died on the cross as the unblemished lamb and perfect sacrifice, everything changed. In His death, Jesus fulfilled everything He came to do in His life. The sacrificial system was no longer necessary. The priesthood was no longer necessary. God had warned Adam and Eve that sin would end in death. The first Adam failed. Jesus, the perfect Adam was faithful. Sin did end in death. Jesus' death buried our sin forever.

Read Isaiah 53. Use the space below to write words or phrases that stir your feelings of sorrow over sin and gratitude for Jesus' ultimate sacrifice.

Purpose in Our Pain

Jesus' final words from the cross were "It is finished," (John 19:30). But that was 2000 years ago. Why then did the story not end there? Or with His resurrection three days later? Or at least with His ascension from earth into heaven 40 days later? Why add the step of sending the Holy Spirit? Why does human history continue to plow along like a runaway train? Why does a good God allow suffering to continue moment after moment, day after day, year after year, generation after generation. What is He waiting for?

If you've ever wondered about any of those things, you're not the first. In one of his letters Peter, answered this question. People were already (and understandably) eager for Jesus to return and complete this ministry of reconciliation. They wanted God to make everything right again, bring it all back into order, and experience the peace of His presence forever. Although if you think about it, if God would have ended the story before now, you wouldn't be here. It's easy to get impatient once you're part of the in-crowd, so to speak. It's kind of like when you were a kid playing musical chairs and you wanted the music to end as long as you had a seat, but who cares about anyone else, right?

Read 2 Peter 3:9.

Because Jesus was perfect, His sacrifice was the only one that could reconcile us to God and bring true healing. As we experience His healing God reveals a new purpose in our pain. Our wounds become scars. Our scars become stories. And people need to hear your story. People need to hear His story.

When and about what have you been impatient with God?

What is something that you didn't understand at the time but later saw how God used it for good in your life or in someone else's life?

Read Romans 8:28.

Notice that verse doesn't say everything is good. Although God is good, the world is full of hurtful, painful things. But God can and does use even bad or painful things to accomplish good things for the good of those who love Him and are called according to His purpose.

Yes, we're blessed and we have hope and joy in Christ, but we don't have to pretend that we never hurt or experience hardship. Most people who act this way have either never cared enough about anything to be hurt or, more likely, are hiding from pain.

How do you try to hide your wounds?

How is hiding unhealthy for you? How is it unhelpful for others?

Like Adam and Eve, God is calling you out of hiding your sin also. You can't cover your shame. Only the grace of God and the sacrifice of Jesus can clothe you in His righteousness. It's human nature to try and pass the blame. Adam and Eve tried after the first sin. But God didn't accept their excuses then and He won't except yours today. You're responsible for your own sin (and for how you react to sin and brokenness around you).

What excuses do you make for sin?

At this point, you might be wondering how we experience healing. Practically speaking, what can you do? What does it look like to come out of hiding and stop making excuses?

Confess your sins to God and to other people in your church family. Be honest about being happy, being sad, or needing prayer. Pray and keep praying until God works according to His timing. Do all of these things so that other people can be saved from their sins too (Jas. 5:13-20).

Jesus' suffering enabled Him to help us.

Read Hebrews 2:18.

This is true of the wounds and scars we bear too. The hurt and healing we experience tell the gospel story to others, helping us relate to them in a deeply meaningful way so that they can ultimately understand that their true need is spiritual—they need Jesus.

Read 2 Corinthians 1:3-7.

If you're reading this, you're conscious, your heart and mind are working, blood is still pumping through your veins, and breath is still filling your lungs. That means there's still time to repent right now, believe in Jesus, and be healed. The same is true for the people around you.

You have wounds. Jesus has healing. You have scars. People need the story.

Use the space below to list ways Jesus has healed your areas of hurt, guilt, and shame.

Practice telling the story of how your life has been changed by the good news of Jesus.

SESSION FIVE

IDENTITY

In the Christian life, identity has to come before activity.

START

Session 4 focused on how Jesus turns painful wounds into scars that tell a story.

What was most helpful, encouraging, or challenging from your personal reading and reflection in Session 4?

Today we'll shift our from what our scars say about Jesus to what Jesus says about us.

What nicknames have you had and how did you get them?

Do you like your name or any of your nicknames? Why or why not? Briefly share names and answers.

How our identity is defined is more important than we may realize. Keep the following question in mind as we watch the next video.

Who or what defines your true identity?

WATCH

Use the space below to take notes as you watch the video for Session 5.

 CONSIDER THIS

) Through Jesus we can embrace our true identity in Him rather than the false identity sin creates for us.

) Jesus paid the price for our sin and took on our broken identity so that we could experience the life He has for us.

) Jesus identified Himself through baptism before He began His ministry. In the Christian life, identity has to come before activity.

) We must allow the voice of the Father to drown out all the other voices that try to speak into our lives.

 REMEMBER THIS

)

)

)

)

 LOOK THIS UP

) John 11:25
) 1 Corinthians 15
) Matthew 3:13-17
) 1 Samuel 16:13
) Mark 1:9-15
) Luke 15:11-24
) 1 Kings 19

ENCOUNTER

When have you had a hard time discerning God's voice? Why did you want to hear from Him?

Read 1 Kings 19:9-18

In this story, how did God speak to Elijah?

When have you wanted God to speak or act in a powerful way, but He didn't do things the way you expected?

In what ways did God reassure Elijah that He was not alone?

When have you felt alone, especially as a Christian?

Read Matthew 3:13-17.

Why is it significant that God's voice of approval and Jesus identity came before He began doing miracles and ministry? What does this reveal about God? About your relationship with Him? Your identity?

For those who have been baptized, what significance did that act have in your life? Why were you baptized? If you haven't yet been baptized, what keeps you from being baptized?

RESPOND

Jeff pointed out that you can't hear a whisper unless you tune your ear to it. What are some ways you can tune your ear to hear God more clearly?

How can you help others in the group be more tuned to hearing God speak?

On the following pages are three days of personal reading and reflection. Complete these before your next group session.

PERSONAL READING AND REFLECTION

When God Whispers

Review these three major points from the last session:

> We all have wounds. Some of these are self-inflicted by our own sin, other times we are injured by others' sin, and we all experience pain and suffering in a broken world.

> Our God doesn't just know about our suffering; He knows what it feels like to suffer. Jesus was tempted and hurt, getting the full human experience but He never sinned.

> Because Jesus was perfect, His sacrifice was the only one that could reconcile us to God and bring true healing. As we experience His healing God reveals a new purpose in our pain. Our wounds become scars which tell a story of healing and salvation.

It's helpful to remember that the people in the Bible were real people. Yes, they experienced God in amazing and sometimes supernatural ways, but they were ordinary people. The extraordinary and miraculous events we read about were written down because they are so extraordinary and miraculous. It was not the everyday experience of every person who ever loved God to miraculously see and hear God.

That wasn't even the everyday experience for people like Abraham, Moses, the prophets, or even Jesus' disciple. Of course the disciples saw God everyday when they were with Jesus, but they didn't realize He was God at the time and surely some days were pretty normal. After all, Jesus was constantly explaining things or reminding them about what He just said or did.

They were real people with real thoughts, emotions, and concerns.

So to be encouraged, let's look at two guys spread out over history who didn't quite know what to do when life wasn't meeting their expectations and neither was God. Then we'll look at two women who have a great lesson for us.

Read 1 Kings 19:1-18.

When have you felt alone, especially as a Christian?

When has doing the right thing and trusting God seemed to make life harder instead of easier?

We've all heard the stories, or testimonies, about how someone lived a crazy life and then met Jesus and everything was happily ever after. But for most of us, living by faith doesn't make things look better. Sometimes it seems to make things worse.

In this Scripture passage, Elijah sure doesn't look like one of the most famous prophets in history. He's falling asleep depressed and overwhelmed to the point of wishing he was dead. He's running scared from a woman he angered. He's ignoring God's miraculous provision but worried about being killed. And finally he's whining about being all alone when God informs him that there's actually 7,000 people who have remained faithful. That's 7,000 nameless people who don't have their stories written down but God sees them.

Previously, Elijah experienced God's power by changing the weather, been miraculously fed in several different ways, called down fire from heaven in a religious showdown and raised a little boy back to life for a kind widow. Wow. It's no wonder he was at the end of his rope but has also grown used to God working in big and impressive ways.

When have you wanted God to show up in a big way but instead you got a whisper?

We've already seen in this study that being with Jesus didn't necessarily make things easier to understand or believe. Check out Thomas' story of needing Jesus to show up.

Read John 20:24-29.

Imagine what Thomas is experiencing before Jesus shows up. The other disciples say they've all seen Jesus. If it was true, why didn't he get to experience it? Why would they make something like that up? Did Jesus not care about him as much as He cared about the others? Were they messing with him in some cruel way as he grieved the death of someone he was close to? What on earth was going on? What should he believe?

What's most encouraging to you about the way Jesus responded to Thomas? Why is that encouraging?

When have you struggled to believe something about Jesus?

Or with what questions about Jesus do you still wrestle?

How has Jesus met you in your doubt and helped you believe?

This disciple got stuck with the unfortunate nickname of Doubting Thomas. We still use that phrase for skeptics. But one of the greatest parts of this story, one that's often overlooked, is how Thomas responds after Jesus shows Thomas His scars. (Scars really do tell great stories that can bring people to faith!)

Thomas responded to Him, "My Lord and my God!" (John 20:28)

How can you worship Jesus personally, even when you don't fully understand God?

Finally, let's look at a quick story of two sisters.

Read Luke 10:38-42.

Write a summary of what each sister was doing. Put a star next to the one Jesus said made the right decision in that moment.
  > **Mary:**

  > **Martha:**

It's easy, especially in this generation, to think that you always have to be doing something meaningful, and by meaningful I mean some epic adventure or sacrificial service. But sometimes all you need to do is sit at the feet of Jesus and quietly listen as He whispers. Spend time right now just being quiet and still.

DAY TWO

Earning Your Identity

Your wage is what you earn from your work. It's the fruit of your labor, so to speak. No matter how much somebody likes you or not, there's a legal obligation to pay workers their wages.

Look at what the Bible says about the payment you've earned each time you've chosen to do things your own way instead of trusting your Creator and King.

Read Romans 6:23.

The bare minimum you're owed is death. These words have echoed throughout the pages of history since the first man and woman sinned. God warned them that the payment for sin was death but they didn't believe that God's instruction was best for them. In the context of this verse in Romans, there's a metaphor explaining that when you sin, you're choosing to work for sin. You're a slave and sin is your master. That master is cruel and abusive and punishing but the payment is fair. The payment you are legally owed is death.

That's a sobering reality. You deserve death. You've earned it. That's the bad news.

But the good news—the gospel—is that God is a good master. King of kings. He freely offers the gift of eternal life through faith in Christ Jesus our Lord.

It's easy to start thinking that somehow God owes us and we deserve something from Him. But notice that verse doesn't say that we work for Him now. It says He gave us a gift. Why? Because He loves you. He doesn't have to, but He does. He chooses to love you.

Have you ever felt God owed you something for good behavior? Explain.

Believing God will give you good things if you're good and bad things if you're bad is believing that you can manipulate God. That's not a relationship, that's a vending machine, or a cosmic robot at best.

That's not Christianity, that's a pagan idea. That's what those guys Elijah battled on Mount Carmel believed when they acted crazily hoping their god would send fire down from heaven. It never came.

Do you believe that God is more or less pleased with you based on your behavior?   Yes   No

Do you believe that God is more or less likely to give you what you want based on your behavior?   Yes   No

Jesus gave us something infinitely better than religious hoops to jump through to earn God's favor. He introduced the world to a personal relationship with a loving Father.

One of the best stories in Scripture to illustrate the scandalous love of God is The Parable of the Lost Son in Luke 15.

Read Luke 15:11-32.

Jesus was telling this parable to the Pharisees—the religious elite who thought they deserved God's blessings. They were the older son, who was just as lost as the younger son who wasted his inheritance on sinful living. The older son hated the idea of the father being gracious toward the wildly immoral younger son. The older son felt like the father owed him more than the younger son because he had always kept the rules.

Usually this story is told for the sake of those who identify with the younger son. He knew he had been selfish and stupid. He could easily see the painful situation that he had gotten himself into by choosing a life apart from his father.

It's easy to spot the sins of people caught up in self-indulgence and immoral living. It's a lot harder to recognize the sins of people caught up in self-righteousness, legalism, and moral comparison.

Both sons took their father for granted. Both sons just wanted the blessings and benefits of their father without enjoying his presence and a relationship with him. Both sons were lost. But only the younger son confessed and repented, coming back to the father. The father was full of compassion as he welcomed his son home.

On the scale below, with one end being "ashamed: rock bottom in the pigpen" and the other being "arrogant: looking down from a moral pedestal," circle your most recent condition.

ASHAMED |———————+———————+———————+———————| ARROGANT

Which son do you most often resemble—the younger, immoral son or the older, judgmental son? Explain your answer.

In what are you seeking your identity? Experience? Pleasure? Wealth? Ability? Morality? Other:

If you have a hard time knowing where your sense of identity comes from, ask yourself what you couldn't be happy without.

What makes you angriest? What makes you happiest?

The older son got angry because his whole system of ideals, how life worked, and his sense of identity and value came crashing down. When his father didn't show him special treatment due to his better behavior (or at least what that son considered better behavior) he didn't know what to do and was left standing outside of the party. But the father gave both of them the choice to enjoy his generous love.

Read Galatians 4:4-7

What do these verses say about your identity? Circle key words.

What does that passage say about your ability to work for God (and to earn His approval)?

Spend a few minutes thanking God for adopting you into His family, welcoming you with open arms, and giving you the free gift of an inheritance in His kingdom.

Back to the Future

Throughout this study, we've been looking at what the Bible says about how we live each day knowing the end of the story. Well, technically the story goes on forever, but what we mean is that God will ultimately restore all things, bringing everything back into alignment. But until that day comes, we are at the point of overlap.

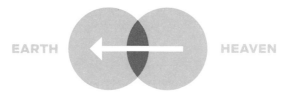

As Christians, we live out our future reality in the present. We live on earth as citizens and heirs of the kingdom of heaven. We leave the old in the past and live in our future identity.

Read Ephesians 4:22-24.

We get a glimpse of this transformation from old to new in baptism. It testifies to our identity in Christ and the family of God.

Read Romans 6:4.

It's like traveling through time. Baptism is a before and after picture. Past, present, and future are all tied up in that moment.

Have you been baptized?   Yes   No

If so, describe when, where, and who was there.

Why was it a significant experience for you?

Read Romans 6:1-11. Summarize the meaning of baptism described here:

All this talk about death might sound morbid at first. But it's actually a really beautiful and hopeful picture of rebirth and resurrection.

In baptism you are identifying with the Son of God, joining His family, and enjoying life as His co-heir. You get to hear the same voice spoken over you as Jesus heard.

Read Matthew 3:16-17.

How much would it mean to you to know without a doubt that God was pleased with you?

NOTHING ├────────────┼────────────┼────────────┤ EVERYTHING

Don't miss this. This is huge. The voice of God our Father declared His pleasure with Jesus before He had performed one miracle, taught one thing, or had died on the cross.

God's delight in Jesus was based solely on His identity. His love was based on their relationship as Father and Son.

The exact same thing is true for you too. God's delight in you is based solely on your identity. His love is based on your relationship as Father and child of God.

Once again, we're not just talking about an abstract picture. The Bible gives practical takeaways for how to live out your resurrected identity as a child of God and coheir with Christ.

Read Colossians 3:1-17.

On the left, write the negative things to put to death.

On the right, write the positive things to put on.

OLD SELF | NEW SELF

Use these lists in your prayer time. Ask for God's grace in helping you put to death your old self and to do everything in the name of Jesus.

Finally, read Romans 8:1-4, 14-17, 35-39, as a prayerful act of worship, letting God speak to you through His Word.

If you're willing, read it aloud, especially verses 35-39 so that you can literally listen to the word of your heavenly Father assuring you of His unconditional love and your freedom as His child.

TABLE

The table is that place where heaven and earth collide, a glimpse at the future Jesus has for all those who follow Him.

START

Session 5 focused on our identity in Jesus.

What was most helpful, encouraging, or challenging from your personal reading and reflection in Session 5?

Today we'll wrap everything up in what may be a surprising topic.

What's the best meal you've ever had and what made it so great?

As we wrap up this study, keep the following question in mind.

How does my life tell the story of a God who wants us to enjoy abundant life now, not just eternal life in heaven?

WATCH

Use the space below to take notes as you watch the video for Session 6.

CONSIDER THIS

- We can't help but want to share our lives with others. It is how God designed us.

- The table represents that place we are willing to open up and share our lives and issues with others.

- Transformation, learning, and understanding happens at the table (Luke 24:13-32).

- Jesus constantly connected everyday life to biblical truth.

- The table is that place where heaven and earth collide, a glimpse at the future Jesus has for all those who follow Him (Rev. 19:6-9).

REMEMBER THIS

-

-

-

-

-

LOOK THIS UP

- Luke 5:30-31; 22:1-38; 24:13-32
- Revelation 19:6-9

ENCOUNTER

How did Jeff say that the table was a connecting point for everything we've discussed over the past sessions?

How would you summarize the significance of rest and community?

Read Luke 22:14-20.

The Passover meal was originally celebrated to remember how God miraculously saved the Israelites from slavery, establishing them as a unique people free and set apart from the rest of the world with God as their King. How did Jesus give this specific meal new meaning? How does the original meaning help you understand what Jesus was doing?

Read Luke 24:13-35.

How does this story reveal that all of Scripture, even the Old Testament, is a story about Jesus?

How does this story reveal that being taught about Jesus and the Bible is a good starting point, but not the same as truly knowing Jesus?

How does Jesus use the meal to reveal the truth of His identity?

What else was most helpful, encouraging, or challenging for you in the video? Why?

What has been most helpful, encouraging, or challenging during this study?

RESPOND

What will be your greatest takeaway from this study?

Jeff intended to show us that being a Christian is about so much more than just going to heaven when you die; so what would you now say about the Christian life?

On the following pages are three days of personal reading and reflection. Complete these before your next group session.

PERSONAL READING AND REFLECTION

Eat, Drink, and Remember

DAY ONE

Let's review the following three major points from last session before moving forward:

> God speaks in the ordinary as well as in the epic.
> God doesn't owe us anything, but lavishes scandalous love upon us to make us a part of His family.
> God's delight in us is based on identity, not performance.

After a short ministry of about three years with His disciples, right before Jesus was betrayed, arrested, tried, beaten, mocked, and executed, He knew what was about to happen and Jesus did something amazing.

If it were me, and I knew what was about to happen and that these guys were about to begin the greatest work and most important mission the world has ever known—a movement that literally changed the course of human history—I'd be having a cram session to make sure everybody knew their role. We'd go over key teaching, strategy, whatever.

But Jesus doesn't do this. Yes, He gathered His closest friends. And Yes, He provided some instruction, but not in a way that anybody expected. Jesus, the Son of God, just hours before He's betrayed by a close companion and murdered for crimes He didn't commit, sits down and has a meal.

Read Luke 22:7-23.

Describe the tone of Jesus and the atmosphere at this scene.

What does the fact that Jesus took time to share this meal with His disciples say to you about its significance?

What does it say to you about Jesus that He shared this time with Judas, knowing the plan for betrayal?

Some pretty amazing things are taking place in this story. First, how Peter and John were supposed to secure the room for the Passover was pretty incredible. No names are given. No address is given. Just find a guy, go to that house, and ask for the room.

And that's what happens. Peter and John find the guy, follow him, and secure the place for the Passover to be observed. That's a small miracle all by itself. Add to that equation the fact that carrying water was almost always a chore done by women makes the guy a little easier to identify but makes Jesus' awareness of the extraordinary detail even more miraculous.

Then, the Passover meal itself was so significant.

Read Exodus 12:2.

The observance of Passover would remind God's people of a new beginning in their lives. The calendar would literally start over with this significant event.

Why did our calendar reset with a starting point of just over 2000 years ago? What do B.C. and A.D. refer to in our calendar today?

Whether people choose to worship Jesus or not, He literally changed history and is the life around which all history now revolves. Everything is measured in relation to Him.

Read Exodus 12:5-7.

What was to be killed in observance of Passover?

Notice the communal nature of what is happening. There was a collective responsibility for killing the Passover lamb. The blood of the lamb was then to be spread on the wooden posts of each doorway.

Read Exodus 12:12-13.

What was judgment (death) or salvation dependent upon?

Read Exodus 12:24-28.

Why is it called Passover?

How does this story point to Jesus' death on the cross?

This would not have been the first time Jesus observed the Passover with His disciples. But on this occasion, He gave new significance to this important meal.

Read Luke 22:19-20.

God's people had been commanded by God to observe this meal in remembrance of the deliverance from Egypt He had provided. When Jesus said to now remember Him, He was saying that He was God, He was the one providing true salvation, and by His blood alone would the judgment of death pass over someone. Jesus' words would have been considered radical and even blasphemous ... unless they were true.

Within hours, Jesus was betrayed. He was killed as the perfect lamb of God. His body was broken and His blood poured out. All of history would be reset and measured by His life. Only through faith would someone enter into the community of God's people.

Today we live according to the new covenant that Jesus proclaimed with the cup.

Read Jeremiah 31:31-34.

Thank God for putting this new law in your heart, freeing you from sin, judgment, death. Because of Jesus, you can know God.

Be Still

As a culture, it seems like many of us have lost the art of unplugging and simply being in the moment. We're addicted to knowing what's going on somewhere else and to letting people know what we're doing, even if it's simply eating a meal or enjoying a cup of coffee.

Now, social media is a great thing. We have tons of information at our fingertips and we can stay in touch with and get to know people all over the world in ways we never could before.

Although we've missed the point a little bit, this shows that there is a desire in us for connection and relationship. We understand from the Scripture that this was God's design from the beginning. Let's go back to Genesis again to look at three things God said "in the beginning ... "

First, do you remember, the pattern in creation of "it was good" after each day? There's something fascinating about the fact that even before sin enters the world there's something that God says "is not good."

Read Genesis 2:15-25.

What's the first thing God says is not good (See verse 18.)?

What two words are used to describe woman in relation to man?

There's this beautiful picture of Adam breaking out into song when he sees Eve for the first time. (Notice in verse 23 how the text is indented. Its probably formatted this way to indicate that it is poetry.) Adam gets all romantic when he sees the first woman and we have the world's first marriage. Eve is called his wife in Genesis 2:24-25.

Now, obviously this doesn't mean that God thinks we should never be alone. However, what it does mean is that, like God who exists as Father, Son, and Holy Spirit, and everything else in creation that has a counterpart, God created human beings to be in relationship. We're made for community.

What distracts you from real, meaningful relationships?

How can you be intentional about developing meaningful relationships?

Who are your closest relationships?

Do they encourage you in your relationship with God?

Notice that Eve is also called Adam's helper. That's not a demeaning term. Before God said it isn't good for man to be alone, God had given man work to do. Understand that work wasn't the punishment for the fall. Toilsome work was the punishment. (See Genesis 3:17-19). God created man and woman to joyfully participate in satisfying and meaningful work. As those uniquely created in His image and likeness, God gave them authority over all of His creation.

Think back to the last session when you read Colossians 3:1-17. We see there that in Christ, we're being restored to this picture of God's design in the garden. The image of God is being renewed, we're united in one body (symbolically, not physically), we should sing together in praise of God's goodness, and our work should be worshipful and good.

What work do you most enjoy?

How can you honor God in everything you do (even what you may not enjoy so much)?

And finally, look at the last day of creation. God does something else amazing that we often overlook or take granted. Next to our relationship with Him and with each other, it's one of God's greatest gifts.

Read Genesis 2:1-3.

What did God do on the seventh day?

When you hear the word "Sabbath," what do you think?

Sabbath is part of God's rhythm for life. It's more than a religious observance. I don't know exactly what it means for God to rest, but He blessed a day of rest, making it holy before any established religion ever existed.

Not only is rest good for us, but it's also an act of worship. It doesn't have to be a strict, legalistic thing. The point is recognizing that God created and provides everything we need, so we can trust Him to take care of us. If God can rest, then we can rest. It's bad for us to always feel like we have to be busy. In a sense, we're saying we don't trust that we'll be taken care of, have what we need, or be satisfied unless we're always working.

Weirdly enough, worshipful rest is something we have to be intentional about. It may take a little planning or a lot of self control. Apparently, this goes against our nature, because God has to command it. In the Ten Commandments, only Sabbath and idolatry get more than a single verse explaining the importance of that command. (See Ex. 4:8-11.)

Read Hebrews 4:1-11.

How do you carve out time for rest and worship?

What refreshes you?

The Sabbath, a time of worshipful rest, is yet another picture pointing to a bigger and better story. In these verses God is revealing that ultimately only those who have responded to the gospel of Jesus will receive the blessing of holy, worshipful rest forever.

Remember the story of Mary and Martha? Martha thought it was most honoring to rush busily around to work for Jesus. But Jesus said Mary resting at His feet and listening to His words was the best thing to do in that moment. So work is a gift from God, part of His design for our lives, but it has to be balanced with intentional, focused rest. Both work and rest are acts of worship as we follow the example (and command) of God.

> *"Be still, and know that I am God." (Ps. 46:10a ESV)*

Take time to "be still" and rest in God's presence. Commit to intentionally and regularly set apart time to worship God and trust that in His goodness you have everything you need.

A Foretaste of Forever

Read Luke 5:27-32.

Matthew was a tax collector. Tax collectors were not very popular during Jesus' day. They were known to skim a little off the top to keep for themselves. Not only did they get rich off of other people, but they were also seen as working for the Roman empire. Think about the tension and hatred that would get cranked up when a Jew was collecting taxes, keeping some for himself, and giving the rest to the Roman empire.

DAY THREE

Jesus not only ate with this guy and his friends, but He called Matthew to leave everything behind in his old way of life and follow Him into a bigger and better story. The religious establishment didn't like this.

Jesus was clear that in His kingdom, life is about knowing that we need His love and forgiveness so that we can live each day with gratitude. Then we start bringing those little pockets of heaven on earth to everyone in our circle of influence. When that happens, people's lives are transformed, wounds are healed, and sinners are reconciled to God.

Think of ways you can use a meal to share the love of Jesus.

Go ahead and plan at least one meal that you'll invite someone to join you. Maybe even plan a regular time and day of the week to meet someone to build the relationship in a way that encourages you both to grow spiritually.

WHEN: WHERE: WHO:

That's what Christianity is all about. It was always about experiencing God's kingdom on earth as it is in heaven. It's about relationship. It's about growth. It's about life-change. It's so much more than just going to heaven when you die.

But one day, those who know Christ will be with Him for forever. We do look forward to the day when heaven and earth are brought back into alignment. It's just that we don't wait for it. We start living that future reality now. We get little tastes of it here, like appetizers or samples before the great feast. When that day finally comes, it'll look something like the picture we find in Revelation 19:6-8.

Read Revelation 19:6-8.

You may not think of yourself as a saint, but you are. The word saints means "holy ones." When you take off the old self and put on the new self, you are being clothed in the righteousness of Christ. He makes you holy. His love for you cleanses you from sin and impurity and your life becomes the fine linen adorning the bride.

The Bible is clear that marriage is and always has been a picture of Jesus and His bride—the Church. We are the Bride of Christ. You and everyone who believes in Jesus for the forgiveness of sin and a new life are the Church.

> *For this reason a man will leave his father and mother and be joined to his wife, and the two will become one flesh. This mystery is profound but I am talking about Christ and the church. (Eph. 5:31-32)*

Are you seeing this? God's Word says that ever since God created and blessed Adam and Eve, He had a picture of Jesus, you, me and every saint in the Church in mind!

From Genesis to Revelation, the story has been about God reconciling people to Himself.

NEW HEAVEN

NEW EARTH

God will ultimately restore all things, bringing everything back into alignment.

Read Revelation 21:1-7.

Do you see how it all comes around full circle and ties together in the end?

- The story is complete. But goes on forever.
- God dwells with His people. Forever.
- The Kingdom is established. Forever.
- Every wounds is healed. Forever.
- We become children of God. Forever.
- We eat, drink, and live. Forever.

You like weddings? They're usually a big deal. The idea is that they only happen once in a lifetime so the bride and groom look their very best, everyone they love is invited, and the biggest celebration imaginable is thrown in honor of the happy couple. They pledge their faithfulness to one another for the rest of their lives.

This is the picture of eternal life. It is heaven crashing into earth in the most spectacular way imaginable.

Heaven isn't some boring place. It's the perfect union of God's realm and ours. It's the marriage of Christ and the Church. It's the story God has been telling since "In the beginning ... "

It's the picture God painted when presenting the first woman to the first man. And what they broke, He made new. It's the consummation of all things. And all of us who know Christ will enjoy it forever.

NOTES

NOTES